WAVE GOODBYE!

Simple Tsunami Mitigation

John LeRoux

BALBOA.
PRESS

A DIVISION OF HAY HOUSE

Balboa Press books may be ordered through booksellers or by contacting:

Balboa Press
A Division of Hay House
1663 Liberty Drive
Bloomington, IN 47403
www.balboapress.com
1 (877) 407-4847

Because of the dynamic nature of the Internet, any web addresses or links contained in this book may have changed since publication and may no longer be valid. The views expressed in this work are solely those of the author and do not necessarily reflect the views of the publisher, and the publisher hereby disclaims any responsibility for them.

The author of this book does not dispense medical advice or prescribe the use of any technique as a form of treatment for physical, emotional, or medical problems without the advice of a physician, either directly or indirectly. The intent of the author is only to offer information of a general nature to help you in your quest for emotional and spiritual well-being. The author of this particular book is primarily interested in your physical well-being. In the event you use any of the information in this book for yourself, which is your constitutional right, the author and the publisher assume no responsibility for your actions.

Print information available on the last page.

ISBN: 978-1-5043-7841-3 (sc)
ISBN: 978-1-5043-7842-0 (e)

Balboa Press rev. date: 04/19/2017

WAVE GOODBYE!

Simple Tsunami Mitigation

John LeRoux

BALBOA.
PRESS

A DIVISION OF HAY HOUSE

Balboa Press books may be ordered through booksellers or by contacting:

Balboa Press
A Division of Hay House
1663 Liberty Drive
Bloomington, IN 47403
www.balboapress.com
1 (877) 407-4847

Because of the dynamic nature of the Internet, any web addresses or links contained in this book may have changed since publication and may no longer be valid. The views expressed in this work are solely those of the author and do not necessarily reflect the views of the publisher, and the publisher hereby disclaims any responsibility for them.

The author of this book does not dispense medical advice or prescribe the use of any technique as a form of treatment for physical, emotional, or medical problems without the advice of a physician, either directly or indirectly. The intent of the author is only to offer information of a general nature to help you in your quest for emotional and spiritual well-being. The author of this particular book is primarily interested in your physical well-being. In the event you use any of the information in this book for yourself, which is your constitutional right, the author and the publisher assume no responsibility for your actions.

Print information available on the last page.

ISBN: 978-1-5043-7841-3 (sc)
ISBN: 978-1-5043-7842-0 (e)

Balboa Press rev. date: 04/19/2017

"I dream things that never were and I say, why not?"
-George Bernard Shaw

PREFACE

There is a common belief that you can't stop a tsunami. What if this belief IS NOT TRUE?

After much thought, I've concluded that the mayhem caused by tsunami waves can be prevented with today's technology. The method considered in this book is simply placing air, or some other gas, ahead of the wave while it's still in deep water. In the following pages, I will show that this method is a logical and effective way to stop or weaken tsunami waves before they can do any damage.

I've often seen the word "impossible" used regarding stopping tsunamis. No one truly believes that this an impossible dream. Many billions of dollars are spent worldwide every year to build and maintain seawalls and floodgates. We build these hoping we never need to use them. When they are needed they sometimes work and sometimes don't. Even when allowed to run their course, tsunamis are stopped eventually by Mother Nature. Often, they'll stop before they do much damage, owing to the particulars of a given situation. I've heard scientists remark that the reef absorbed much of the energy of a tsunami, so while we who are on the shore escaped devastation, the reef didn't fare so well. If a reef can mitigate tsunami damage, why can't man? It's reasonable to assume that if there were a simple, inexpensive way to prevent tsunami destruction someone would have thought of it by now. We don't need some retired letter carrier (yours truly) to tell us we've been wasting billions on seawalls. On the off chance that I'm right, and the untried mitigation methods listed in this book *do* work, the benefits to the world could be immeasurable. In fact, even if they work just a little bit, (and I don't see how they couldn't) significant mitigation could be brought about by upping the scale of the technique.

Thomas Edison didn't invent the light bulb. There were inferior inventions for 75 years before he created a commercially viable bulb. With this book, I hope to fill the role of the person who told Edison that a light bulb was possible. Whoever he was.

CONTENTS

CHAPTER ONE

The Set-Up

Spoiler Alert

This entire book is summarized in the preface. For the reader who would like a little more substance as to the contents and conclusion of this book I'll provide that now:

This book begins with its conclusion: Tsunamis can be stopped at sea. The rest of the book merely explains the reason this is true and methods to accomplish this. I'll start with some disclaimers about my lack of credentials and the absence of a scientific study on this concept. Next, I'll provide a layman's understanding of waves in general and tsunamis specifically. I'll then present a short discourse on the current procedures being used to mitigate tsunami damage. For some readers, the following section on the origin and development of this idea might be interesting. I'll then present the theory behind the concept, as well as some concrete ideas on ways to implement this theory in the real world. I'll wrap up the book with some thoughts about the potential of this concept, and an apology for not writing a better book sooner. So, let's get started!

The Birth of an Idea

When the Indian Ocean tsunami happened in December of 2004 the world was shocked. Hundreds of thousands of people were killed in a single day. I wondered how such a tragedy could spring from an earthquake hundreds of miles off shore and 30 kilometers below sea level. A pebble tossed into a pond creates circular ripples. A disturbance under the ocean should cause a wave shaped as a ring. Once the radius of the ring is 5 miles its circumference is just over 31 miles. When this circular wave travels 100 miles from its source the circumference is 628 miles. You would think that the intensity of the wave would shrink as the circumference grew. This way of thinking was one dimensional, and not making use of the metric system. I then did some two-dimensional thinking, as the wave would cover a large expanse of ocean. At 4000 meters of depth the wave would be a circular ring with a radius of 213 kilometers (see figure 3). Therefore, it would cover over 142,000 square kilometers when it first came into being. After the outer edge of the wave has moved out 639 kilometers from its original location it's nothing but a 213-kilometer-wide ring encircling its point of origin. That ring will cover 1,019,180 square kilometers of ocean. The area of the wave has increased by a factor of 7! How can a force causing havoc close to its origin cause similar problems over an area 7 times as large? Thinking in three dimensions shed some light on the issue, but the ratio remained the same.

Since the size of the wave doesn't directly correlate with its potential for damage, something else is going on. After all, a high tide travels around the world nearly every day, looking much like a wave, and no unexpected problems occur on the world's coasts. If we were looking at a high tide from space, we would see a bulge in the earth's oceans of perhaps two meters in height generally traveling east to west at nearly the speed of the earth's rotation. After further study I've discovered that some of this view of tides is probably wrong, but the point is tides move fast and are predictable on shore. Interestingly, if you left a sealed bottle with a bit of air in the water at high tide and looked for it a day later, you'd realize the tide travelled around the world while the bottle barely budged.

The thing that explains the difference between a tsunami wave and a normal high tide is horizontal movement, or more simply, energy flow. While a tide is primarily the Moon's gravity lifting the sea minutely away from the globe, a tsunami is caused by a tremendous energy transfer, from the disturbance outward. The tsunami's energy transfer is similar to what we see in a tube, a tub or a lake, where once the vessel is at capacity, the outflow equals the inflow.

My Theory—Tides Versus Tsunamis

It is widely understood that tides are caused by the gravitational pull of the Moon and the Sun on the Earth's oceans, with the Moon having more effect than the Sun. There are two high tides every day. The higher of the two generally follows the Moon on its orbit around the Earth. The second high tide is on the opposite side of the Earth than the slightly larger tide. I believe the smaller high tide is caused by the Moon/Earth orbiting duo. The center of gravity of this pair is somewhere between the Earth and the Moon. The centrifugal force of the Earth's rotation alone is roughly equal around the equator. The centrifugal force of the Moon's orbit pulls fluid away from the center of gravity. While the Earth's gravity is pulling the Moon toward Earth, the Moon's gravity is pulling

3

the Earth toward the Moon. This interplay of forces makes the Earth have a bit of a wobble in its orbit around the Sun. It also causes a tidal bulge on the side of the Earth away from the Moon. If the Moon had an ocean it would also have tides toward and away from the Earth. A high tide can lift the sea level by 10 meters or more in some places. This is a daily occurrence and cannot be considered dangerous. Tides move the ocean's water up and down without adding or subtracting water from the sea. High tides pull water from every direction creating lower tides in the distance. Since the slight flow causing the bulge is from many directions, the tides are neutral in direction. You couldn't ride a high tide around the world in half a day.

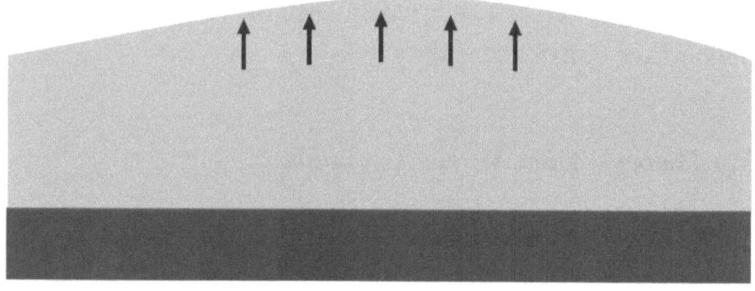

Figure 1—Energy Flow into a High Tide

A tsunami wave can be more dangerous. The amount of water moved in a tsunami is miniscule compared to the movement of water in tides. For instance, one high tide lasts over 6 hours, while one tsunami wave lasts 18 minutes. Both events appear as the surface of the ocean bobbing up and down. A tsunami carries a small amount of lateral energy. This energy comes from one direction and causes a bulge in the water. Theoretically you could surf the wave at certain points, but I wouldn't recommend trying. When the lateral push of a tsunami wave is in the deep ocean, it is widely dispersed. I estimate a ½ meter high wave, covering millions of square kilometers of ocean surface, would have enough lateral energy to destroy a coast. When a tide approaches a shore it's pulling water from the deep ocean behind it. There is no water on the beach to pull into the high tide. In addition, most of the bulge of the high tide is still at sea and rises along the coast gradually. When a tsunami approaches a beach its lateral energy becomes concentrated. The wavelength shrinks and the depth shrinks. (see figure 3) The total lateral energy remains the same. A 50-centimeter wave in the ocean can become a 15-meter wave on the shore.

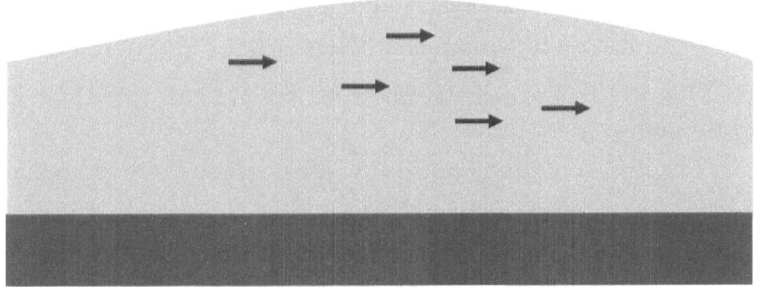

Figure 2—Energy Flow in a Tsunami

After much thought, I came to the conclusion that if we could make the gentle, widely dispersed open ocean tsunami energy transfer less efficient, the result would be weaker waves hitting the shore.

I considered many ways to disrupt the deep ocean energy flow. Bubble wrap, plywood, ramps to bring the wave to the surface prematurely and artificial underwater canyons all crossed my mind. I finally settled on the idea of releasing air or some other gas from the ocean floor ahead of the wave to sap the lateral energy.

About This Book

I've thought a lot about tsunamis in the past years and have come up with my own way of looking at things. You will find several of these observations in this book under the heading: My Theory. These mental images could be close to what credentialed scientists have learned about a particular situation, or they could be way off base. Either way, these observations help me visualize a certain phenomenon without getting hung up on the complex details. My conclusions are not based on an intimate understanding of all the forces involved in earthquakes and tsunamis. I believe a basic idea of the forces at work is sufficient to consider as plausible the simple idea presented in these pages.

The ideas presented in this book have been observed before by anyone giving them a thought. For instance, a tsunami cannot put more water on the land than was disturbed by the quake in the first place. There's no literature on this truism, but I cannot imagine how that statement could be false.

I believe I can persuade open minded people that there is a simple way to weaken tsunamis.

CHAPTER TWO

This is Not a Science Book

Tsunamis are among the most destructive and deadly forces in nature. In recent memory tsunamis have killed hundreds of thousands of people and destroyed trillions of dollars in property. The current approach to mitigating tsunami damage is about the same as it has been for centuries: Building seawalls and encouraging evacuation. Although climate science has been able to estimate potential sea level rise two centuries from now, and what we can do about it, it has been less confident about suggestions to mitigate tsunamis which could occur at any time. Japan has undertaken a $6.8 billion project to build 250 miles of seawalls, which equals about $27 million per mile. My understanding is that 95% of the seawalls in Japan failed during the 2011 tsunami. This book is an attempt to look at tsunami mitigation in a different way, a way which doesn't rely on 2 millennia old technology.

Disclaimers and Generalizations

This book is not a scientific study, and I am not a scientist. Rather, I'm an average person who knows a bit about math and a bit about physics. I'm also fairly good at spacial perception. I've read quite a bit about tsunamis and would like to relate my interpretation of that information to average intelligent people who really haven't thought much about this topic.

In the pages that follow I will be using the metric system. I do that because converting water weight to water volume is simple. Frankly, I am more comfortable with the English system and will sometimes backslide and use it! I will use widely known conversion factors and will ignore the minute differences between shorthand calculations and precise numbers which could be affected by salinity, barometric pressure, temperature and possibly other variables. I will also use simple math to make my point, math which anyone with a calculator can duplicate. I will also use estimates, educated guesses and wild guesses to illustrate concepts. These won't have any substantial influence on my main point. I plan to introduce information, gleaned from many sources without providing attribution. For example, I might say a large tsunami occurred in the Indian Ocean on December 26, 2004, but I won't cite a source. I do this to keep this project simple.

Well Known Numbers

On the following page is a chart which shows the velocity and size of a tsunami wave in various depths of ocean. Seeing this chart really got me thinking about the dynamics of a tsunami wave. I noticed that at 7000 meters the wave traveled at 943 kilometers per hour (about 585 mph). I wondered how you could get water traveling at that speed. I came up with a mental image to help me understand this. If you hammer a nail into a block of wood, the hammer moves at perhaps 40 mph. The nail moves at the same speed, but the energy from the hammer to the nail head to the nail point moves nearly instantaneously, perhaps at 943 kilometers per hour. In a tsunami the same holds true, only the hammer, the nail and the wood are all made of water!

Here is a famous chart of tsunami wave velocity and wavelength for various depths of ocean. With this chart and a knowledge of ocean depths between a given beach and an earthquake, scientists can estimate very accurately the arrival time of an initial tsunami wave.

Depth/Meters	Velocity/km per hr	Wavelength/km
7000	943	282
4000	713	213
2000	504	151
200	159	48
100	112	34
50	79	23
10	36	10.6
5	25	7.6

Figure 3—Tsunami Velocity and Wavelength

There are other commonly known truisms regarding ocean waves and ocean water in general which will frame this presentation. For instance:

A cubic meter of water contains 1000 liters.

A cubic meter of water weighs 1000 kilograms.

The gravitational acceleration constant can be interpreted as distance equals 9.81 meters per second squared. This means that water or a dense object will fall 9.81 meters in one second, or 39.24 meters in two seconds, and so on. Air or water drag complicates this equation.

The speed of a tsunami is equal to the square root of the product of the depth of the ocean times the constant representing the acceleration due to gravity (9.81 meters per second). In other words, at a depth of 4000 meters the wave will be traveling at 198 meters per second or 713 kilometers an hour.

Figure 3 is a widely available chart of wavelengths of deep ocean waves which provides the theoretical wavelength of tsunamis at various depths. It shows that at 7000 meters the length of the wave is 282 kilometers, and at 200 meters the length is only 48 kilometers. This means that a tsunami wave of whatever size takes about 18 minutes to pass a point in the ocean.

Water pressure is expressed in atmospheres, also known as bars. Shorthand calculations translate 10 meters of depth into one additional bar. The pressure on the surface of the water is 1 atmosphere, named after the atmosphere's air pressure' (about 17.5 pounds per square inch). Therefore, the water pressure at 10 meters of depth is 2 bars and at 20 meters it's 3 bars. These numbers include the atmospheric pressure on the surface.

Boyle's Law states that a volume of gas and the pressure are inversely proportional. This means that a cubic centimeter of gas at 1990 meters of depth (200 bar) becomes a 200-cubic centimeter bubble at the surface.

Henry's Law tells us that there is a proportional relationship to the amount of gas which can be dissolved in a liquid and the pressure being exerted on the gas. In other words, the higher the pressure on the water, the greater the amount of gas it can absorb.

An important idea to consider is that a tsunami wave is not water flowing through the ocean. It is, rather, energy traveling through the water. It's somewhat like a Newton's Cradle, where the energy from the first ball travels through three other balls and lifts the fifth ball in a mirror image of the initial energy. If we know how much the first or last ball weighs, and the speed and distance of the initial or terminal motion, we can figure out the amount of energy that passed through the three balls in the middle of the cradle. When we're trying to figure out the energy being carried by a tsunami wave we know it must be less than the initial energy creating the wave. This can be expressed as the volume of water displaced. We're more concerned with the amount of water flooding a distant shore at the end of the wave. This figure, representing volume, lets us know approximately how much energy made it through the "Newton's Cradle" which is the ocean!

Figure 4—A Newton's Cradle

There are different ways to look at the same facts just to understand concepts. For instance, if we estimate that 15 cubic kilometers of ocean water moves five meters closer to the moon during a high tide, we could calculate that fact as being the equivalent of most of that water remaining in place, but 13 cubic meters of water traveling all the way to the moon's surface. The math is correct, but the concept is ludicrous. Perhaps this example doesn't work for most people.

A more useful way of looking at a fact is to break it down to a smaller sample. If we know that a cubic meter of water weighs a metric ton (1000 kilograms) we know a cubic centimeter weighs 1 gram. That isn't a coincidence. If we know that a kilometer-wide slice of a wave contains 3 million cubic meters of excess energy moving in a single direction, we can deduce that a 1 meter slice of the same wave would contain 3 thousand cubic meters of excess energy. If we know the width and height of the wave we can calculate the excess energy of a single cubic meter.

Why Has No One Thought of This?

Since the Japan tsunami of 2011 I've refined this idea and presented it to friends, acquaintances and strangers (including folks from Shark Tank) and have yet to hear the old Groucho Marx line "that's the most ridiculous thing I've ever hoid!" I have been told that there are people out there who have dedicated their careers to tsunami study and mitigation techniques, so why haven't they considered this idea? I can only say that this idea has only been possible to implement since the modern communications age. Without worldwide earthquake detection technology, global positioning satellites and instant international communications, this idea would have no chance. Perhaps the best minds in the field accepted the common refrain that a tsunami cannot be stopped and turned their attention to improving seawalls and evacuation protocols. More pointedly, this idea is so simple I'm sure other people <u>have</u> come up with it. They either saw the fatal flaw in the reasoning that has escaped me, or they just assumed there was one or someone else would have thought of it. I've not discovered this fatal flaw or found anyone else propounding this idea. If you, dear reader, can spot this central flaw I would love to hear about it before I embarrass myself further. If there is none this idea could well be revolutionary!

I've set up an email address for anyone wishing to correct my math or debunk my theory. It is: tsunamistopper@aol.com

CHAPTER THREE

Understanding Waves

A Layman's View

The most efficient way to move water is to let gravity do the work. When gravity isn't practical, the next best way is to apply a force to the nearby water. That moving water will push or pull the adjacent water toward its destination. For example, drinking straws are more efficient than teaspoons, fire hoses are more efficient than bucket brigades, and in water fights, a water pistol is more efficient than water balloons. When a speedboat creates a wake it only displaces water in its path. The water pushed aside creates a wake which moves the next closest water out of the way. That displaced water displaces its neighboring water. And so on. As the wake moves away from the boat's line of travel, the water originally displaced re-occupies the void left by the now departed speedboat. The second displacement rushes back to its original location. And so on. This wake can look impressive, but within a minute it will be undetectable.

Waves at sea are not different than a boat's wake, except in size. Some force, such as the wind, an earthquake or a meteor, displaces water which starts the wave moving. In the case of a tsunami, the initiating earthquake could have lasted as little as several minutes, but the tsunami might travel for hours. By the time the tsunami wave hits a distant shore, every drop of water between the edge of the wave and the original disturbance is more or less back where it started the day. The actual water that is going to be pushed up on land and cause havoc started the day just off the beach. Importantly, the water which will be pushed up on shore must be significantly less in volume than the water displaced by the original disturbance.

Consider the 2004 Indian Ocean tsunami. It was caused by a 1600-kilometer-long earthquake along a fault hundreds of kilometers from population centers. By the time it hit land it was longer than 1600 kilometers, and was affecting land on all the coasts of the Indian Ocean. Some people estimate that 30 cubic kilometers of water was displaced by the earthquake.

Knowing that tsunamis don't last forever, we can infer that some of this tsunami's energy failed to make it to a shoreline. Part of the wave continued through open water to the Atlantic or Pacific Ocean. The energy that made it to land, primarily Indonesia, caused massive death and destruction.

The Size of the Problem

In order to calculate the wave energy contained in a tsunami wave at sea, let's make a few assumptions and look at a theoretical wave to come up with a number. First, let's assume that a destructive wave has twice as much energy as a harmless wave. This number could be way off, but for this argument it will make no difference. Next, let's assume we're talking about one large tsunami wave. Finally, let's assume the wave loses 5% of its potency every 1000 kilometers. We'll be looking at a 100-kilometer-wide wave to limit the example.

Imagine all of the land along a 100-kilometer (62 mile) coastline were inundated by a tsunami. If the water came 2 kilometers inland and reached 10 meters elevation, it would contain 1 cubic kilometer of water. This would be as destructive as any tsunami in recent memory. I'll estimate that an additional half of a cubic meter would need to be moved into the shallows to support the wave. Not all tsunamis cause damage, so let's multiply that one and a half cubic kilometers by two to estimate the amount of forward energy needed to bring about this disaster.

Since the concept of lateral energy flow is essential to the argument presented in this book, I'll spend a few words and 2 images presenting it.

Just before a tsunami wave hits land there is not an abnormal amount of water on the beach or the land nearby. The wave could come ashore in 3 ways: As a wall of water, as a fast tide initially moving outward, or a gradual, but massive rise of the sea level. No matter which way it begins, the magnitude of the tsunami can be measured by maximum inundation.

Figure 5 represents a slice of shoreline just before a massive tsunami wave hits. It's meant to represent the 3 dimensional space the water from the wave will soon fill.

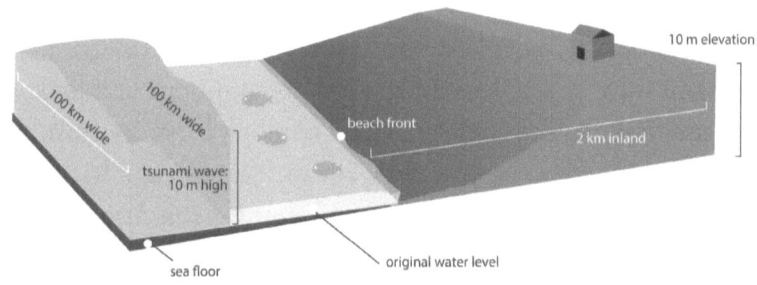

Figure 5—A Section of Beach Before the Wave

There is a finite area that will be filled with water when the wave hits. The total amount of water in the sea will not change with a tsunami. Perhaps a tiny fraction of a percent of the water will be moved onto land for a day or so, but the ocean will not change.

The next image shows the minimum amount of water necessary to create this level of catastrophe on land. Notice I say the minimum. This graphic shows the land being inundated with 1 cubic kilometer of water. We know that the total water movement necessary to achieve this level of inundation must be greater than 1 cubic kilometer. We know, for instance, that the coast can absorb the highest tide of the year with room to spare. We know that for a 10-meter wave to rise up from a 3-meter bay, an additional 7 meters of water must enter the bay. Also, we should consider that while the water is coming up on land it is also flowing back to the sea.

Figure 6 shows the amount of water that needed to spill out of the ocean to inundate a wedge of land 10 meters high, 2 kilometers inland and 100 kilometers wide.

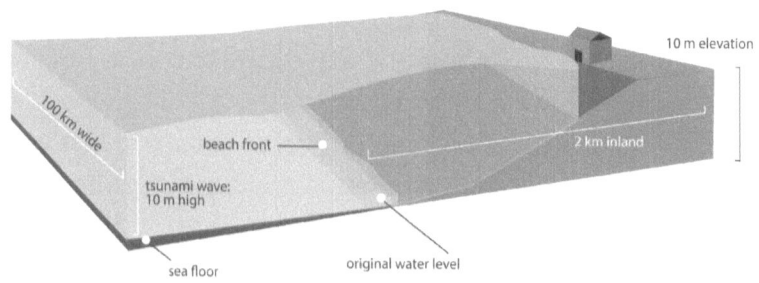

Figure 6—An Inundated Beach

Any reduction of excess energy we can bring to the wave equals a reduction in the amount of water ending up on land. I contend that it is easier and cheaper to prevent 500 million cubic meters of excess lateral wave energy from traveling hundreds of kilometers, than it is to clean up half a cubic kilometer of water from a number of unfortunate seaside communities.

Wave Energy Per Cubic Meter

If there are three cubic kilometers of excess lateral energy in a wave in a 100-kilometer-wide section of deep ocean, it has the potential to cause a catastrophe. At 7000 meters a 100-kilometer-wide section of tsunami wave would involve 197,400 cubic kilometers of ocean (assuming the wave is 282 kilometers from front to back). This means that the forward energy of this wave at sea is approximately 15 ten-thousandths of one percent of all the water in that wave. Since the energy is distributed mostly equally this means that each cubic meter of water has about 15.2 cubic centimeters of forward energy, if interpreted as a fluid equivalent.

Now, here comes the mind-stretching part of this exercise! How would this 3 cubic kilometers of energy, pushing forward at 943 kilometers per hour, be any different than a physical wave moving that much water at that speed? This impossible wave would look like a 1.5-foot-tall pool of water, 62 miles wide and 175 miles from front to back, skimming along the ocean surface at 585 miles per hour! A tsunami wave could appear to be on the surface, as in this example. In reality it involves the ocean from the seafloor to the surface. The telltale sign of a tsunami is a 1 ½- foot tall bulge in the surface height, traveling at 585 miles-per-hour, and lasting for 18 minutes!

Granted, every wave in the ocean was caused by the physical movement of something somewhere. If 50 cubic kilometers of ocean water were to be displaced by something, the repercussions would be widely felt. But after traveling through millions of cubic kilometers of ocean water, the coastline impact could not total anywhere near 50 cubic kilometers. Even 3 cubic kilometers of moving water would have to be dispersed along many kilometers of shoreline. At the shore, quickly moving energy becomes slowly moving water. Like a Newton's Cradle, the only movement noticeable after the initial impact is the movement of the final ball. If 3 cubic kilometers of water does get pushed up on land, it will be the water that started the day just off the beach.

This 3-cubic kilometer mass of water started the day undisturbed just offshore. Sometime earlier, a disturbance of at least 3-cubic kilometers started a wave heading toward this beach. That mass of water quickly pushed the next 3-cubic kilometers out of the way. And so on. The medium through which this energy was passing was millions of cubic kilometers of ocean water. The wave energy was also ocean water, and was indistinguishable from the medium. The wave moved up and down with the center of the wave (and its edges for that matter) moving along at hundreds of kilometers per hour over deep ocean.

When the wave approached land, the amount of water making up the medium lessened. The wavelength shrunk, the velocity slowed and the depth lessened. The forward energy, though, remained the same. When the medium became small enough the energy could no longer be passed along as energy alone. Then it had to start moving some of the water out of the way to make room for that 3 cubic kilometers of energy. Until that point, it was nothing but an energy mass being transferred through a medium at high speed. Near shore, it could no longer be contained by the shrinking medium. It became a wave that all could see.

My Theory—Tsunamis Aren't Noticed at Sea

Imagine a gigantic wave carrying half of the energy of the Indian Ocean tsunami concentrated in a single wave, a mere 100 kilometers wide at 7000 meters of depth. Since the wavelength is 282 kilometers, that 15 cubic kilometers of energy would be dispersed over 28,200 square kilometers of ocean area. That averages to 53 centimeters of sideways pressure for the entire wave. A fish swimming around at 100 meters of depth would suddenly feel like it was swimming at 100.53 meters. Since the wave here is energy, 53 centimeters would not present itself clearly on the surface. I won't guess how much a satellite could detect. At 5 meters of depth the wavelength is only 7.6 kilometers. The 15 cubic kilometers of energy (okay, now it's water) would cover each section of the surface with 19.7 meters of water. It wouldn't take a satellite to notice the wave at this point. It would be impossible for 15 cubic kilometers of water to get into a space 100 kilometers wide, with a wavelength of 7.6 kilometers, and only 5 meters high. That much energy would produce a wave 19.7 meters high.

Modeling a Wave

If this mass of energy behaves like a pulse, or several pulses eighteen minutes apart, we can imagine a strategy to mitigate its destructive power. Every bit of this forward moving energy needs to pass through every plane on its way to a shore in the distance. You can block this progression in a tiny plane of the ocean. It would work the same way as putting a drinking glass over three dominos in a 1000 domino chain, or putting a small sponge between two balls of a Newton's Cradle.

The Ocean is a churning mass of complicated forces. Wind, earthquakes, tributary rivers, the Moon's gravity, the rotation of the Earth and vegetation on the ocean floor are but a few of the factors that affect the living sea. This book will focus on one of these forces, and seek to mitigate the damage the resultant wave can cause as it hits the shore. We should remember that a tsunami wave is not the only force traveling through the ocean, just the largest one.

Now let's imagine a model of a tsunami wave. Suppose you had a very large steel tank with an inflow hose at one end and an outflow hose at the other. If this tank were filled completely and you still wanted to pump water into it, you could do so. However, if you pumped a gallon or a million liters into the inflow hose, the same amount would flow out of the outflow hose.

It would be the same amount but it would be different water. The water flowing out would be the water that sat closest to the outlet. The water coming in would merely displace the water near the inlet, the water near the inlet would displace the water near it, and so on through the tank. The volume of water in the tank would not change, but you could measure the flow across any plane in the tank, from top to bottom between the inlet and outlet, and determine the amount of water flow. You could also measure the flow across a random sample of cubic meters in the tank and derive a close approximation of the entire flow.

Of course, a more accurate estimate of the average flow across the average cubic meter can be calculated by dividing the total outflow by the tank's total volume. For example, a 100 gallon tank with 1 gallon a minute flow would flow 1% of its volume per minute. Every 100 ounces of water in the tank would pass 1 ounce through per minute as well. The volume of water in the tank would not change, but the pressure of the water in the tank would be slightly higher than normal while this flow was in play.

A wave tank, pool, or lake could handle this excess water differently. It could pass that excess forward in a wave. A tsunami doesn't put extra water in the ocean, it merely moves water around.

Living by the ocean, as I do, I've seen innumerable waves. We call the gentle ones that don't break "bumps" and make attempts to utilize the forward energy in our outrigger canoe. I think I've figured how this gentle appearing force can lift so much water for kilometer after kilometer and expend no energy. Some storm far away started this train of waves rolling and there are few things standing between their formation and our canoe. The energy from the leading edge of the bump reaches the stationary water just ahead of it and applies its force. That water has to get out of the way so some of it is pushed up. After the wave energy passes by, the water that was pushed up falls back down a bit, propelling the wave forward. When the wave "breaks" we know its end is near. At this point, the top of the wave falls over the base and starts churning air into the whole wave. This leads to a foamy wave shrinking in size. My assumption is that foamy water can't propel a wave as efficiently as flat water.

When a tsunami wave hits, the first sign often appears as the tide going out quickly. To conceptualize this phenomenon, think of a 20-meter wave of energy being pushed into 15 meters of water. Since that entire 15 meters of shallow water gets involved in the wave and is still insufficient, the wave starts to pull water from beneath the surface to maintain its 20-meter height. Soon, the remaining water ahead of the wave begins to flow downhill to the bottom of the incoming tsunami. At this point the tsunami starts to sound like a freight train, as it has run out of water to involve and turns to sucking in air. The damage about to be inflicted on the shore results from the size of the wave. This chain of waves could be pushing ashore for hours.

This is a good time to note the obvious: As the medium through which the wave is traveling gets smaller, the lateral energy remains the same. As with a water tank being emptied through a hose, where it's difficult to see the flow by looking into the tank but easy by looking at the hose, the enormity of the wave's power is only obvious at the shore. Most of the three cubic kilometers of lateral flow, which was traveling inconspicuously through 4000 meters of water, is still traveling shoreward in water 5 meters deep. Like the final ball in a Newton's Cradle, the last mass of water is going to move noticeably, but unlike the Newton's Cradle, the energy from behind will continue unceasingly for around 18 minutes per wave.

CHAPTER FOUR

A Line in the Sand / Proof of Concept

The Size of the Problem

A tsunami wave is a finite problem. The most damage it can do can be measured in water volume. The way I've chosen to quantify the impact of a tsunami is to estimate the total amount of water moved onto the shore. If that quantity is one cubic kilometer, that entire mass would have flowed over a line in the sand onto the beach. Logically, at least that much lateral energy would have had to cross a line in the sand ten meters out to sea, or 1000 meters, or whatever distance we wish to consider between the shore and the earthquake.

If we could reduce the flow of tsunami energy over any of these lines by one cubic kilometer, we would lessen the impact of that tsunami to zero. Let's now turn our attention to a line, maybe 10 kilometers from shore, at 200 meters of depth. At this depth, the incoming wave is still 100 kilometers wide, 200 meters deep by definition, and calculated to be 48 kilometers from front to back. Its velocity is 159 kilometers per hour. If the feared 3-cubic kilometers (cited earlier) of lateral energy present in this wave can be reduced to 2-cubic kilometers, a calamity can be prevented.

The volume of ocean containing the wave at this point is 960 cubic kilometers. Since we're worried about 3 cubic kilometers of lateral energy, that translates to 0.3125% of any part of that wave.

The best way to grasp this tsunami wave mechanism is to look at a tiny part of the medium through which the wave flows. Let's consider a 1-cubic meter section of water near the ocean floor at 200 meters of depth at the front end of this incoming wave. Before the wave hits there is no unusual energy transfer between this cube and its adjacent cubic kilometers of ocean. The water pressure is around 20 bar for this section and its neighbors. When the tsunami wave reaches our target, it is comprised of three and an eighth extra liters of lateral energy per cubic meter being pushed into any cubic meter in its path. Our targeted cube now finds itself with more water than it can hold, so every drop of water gets pushed against neighboring drops as they're all seeking space. The excess can't go to the side, up or down because the wave has hit all the neighbor cubes. It must push the excess forward. The wave causes that 3-plus liters of excess lateral energy to travel through that cubic meter in 1/44 of a second (at 159 kilometers per hour). By the time the entire wave has gone by, 150-cubic meters of excess lateral energy has traveled through this single cubic meter. This is quite logical, because if you multiply the 150-cubic meters by the depth (200 meters) and the width (100,000 meters) you get the 3 billion-cubic meters, also known as 3-cubic kilometers, that were our original concern.

Unlike the more scholarly texts that explain that "very little" water is moved forward in a tsunami, I'm going to attempt to quantify the forward motion of the wave on a per square meter basis. In the tank used as a tsunami model, some water was flowing in one end and some water out the other. In other words, there was water moving forward. In an example of 1800 liters of flow in a 10,000-cubic meter tank we can easily calculate the lateral flow, if we know the dimensions of the tank. Let's say the tank is 100 meters long, 10 meters high and 10 meters wide. Over 18 minutes, the water formerly at the front edge of the tank would have moved 1.8 centimeters. (1.8 centimeters times 10 meters times 10 meters equals 1800 liters)

In a tank the front edge of water flow would have moved 1 millimeter a minute, or 16 and 2/3 microns per second. Each individual cubic meter of water in a tsunami works like our tank. In our example of a potentially deadly wave we know that "very little" of the water is moving forward.

In 1 cubic meter at 200 meters of depth, 1 meter represents 1/20,000,000 of the area the wave must pass through. Therefore, the 3 billion-cubic meters of lateral energy which we fear, contributes 150-cubic meters of water flow through our targeted cubic meter. This means that from the time the wave first hits this cubic meter we're imagining, to the time the end of the wave leaves it 18 minutes later, 150 cubic meters of lateral energy will have passed through this cube. While the wave has pushed through at 159-kilometers per hour, most of the movement of this cube was up and down. The entire cube is involved in the wave, but the forward movement is imperceptible. At 159-kilometers per hour it would take less than the entire cubic meter to pass ahead that much energy. At that speed, a 2-centimeter hole in the cube would be sufficient for that volume. The entire cube would transfer the same amount of water per distance at .5 kilometers per hour. The bulk of the water in this wave is merely moving up and down.

I realize that there are differences between an ocean wave and a large tank of water. In a tsunami, there is no extra water being poured or pumped into one side. In waves at sea, millions of tonnes of water (or tons for my fellow Americans) can be tossed around in rough weather with no harmful impact to nearby shores. It's only when an unusual event occurs, like a strong earthquake, that this ordinarily benign process of wave flow can become a disaster. I've also read that research done over 100 years ago established that waves aren't just flowing one way. They are actually more like spheres of water spinning, with the tops of the spheres spinning forward, and the bottoms of the spheres moving water back toward where it started. These spinning spheres can be detected throughout the wave. They are said to get smaller as the depth increases.

Intuitively, we know that a slow disturbance in water causes no wave. You can climb into a swimming pool using a ladder or by doing a cannonball to notice the difference. If we can't slow the speed of the initial disturbance, we can try to slow the efficiency of the energy transfer.

Add Some Bubbles

This is the point where we attempt to do something about the developing catastrophe! Suppose we pump five liters of air into the bottom of this targeted cubic meter, either before the wave gets there or while the wave is transiting this space. Putting aside the fact that gases dissolve in water (we can always surpass those limits), we would end up with the equivalent of 5000 single cubic-centimeter bubbles at the bottom of this cubic meter. This would give the incoming lateral wave energy a path of less resistance once it enters the cube. Instead of moving forward at 138 liters per second (the excess lateral energy times the velocity) five liters of the cube's water could fall one centimeter through the bubbles every 3 hundredths of a second (G=9.81 meters per second squared), or around 150 liters per second.

One Bubble Rises One Meter

Here's the math. It's well known that when a bubble or a swimmer rises in water, it's more accurate to say the water fell around her or it, and now occupies the space formerly occupied by the bubble or swimmer. We can estimate the time required for a bubble to "rise" one meter by calculating the time it takes for water to fall 1 centimeter and multiplying that by 100. The formula says that water will fall 981 centimeters per second squared. In order for a gram of water to fall 1 centimeter (1/981st of the 1 second distance) through that bubble it would take a certain number of seconds which, when squared, would yield the fraction 1 over 981. That number of seconds, therefore, is .0319. This number is for 1 centimeter. This means the bubble would rise 1 meter in just over 3 seconds. Note that since all 5000 cubic centimeters of air came in together at the bottom of our observed cube, water would be falling through all 5 liters simultaneously. Thus, with the addition of 5 liters of air, our observed cubic meter will go from transferring 138 liters of lateral flow per second, to dropping over 156 liters per second. While this water is falling, it cannot at the same time be pushing forward. Once that 156 liters per second is knocked out of passing on energy, it must be re-pressurized by the water behind. The pressure it had carried one second earlier will be lost for good. Eventually all of the excess lateral energy of this wave can be neutralized in this way.

Ocean waves are usually not dangerous to the people on shore, owing to their varied sizes and origins. A tsunami wave can be mitigated by varying its intensity and tweaking the direction of the flow.

Let's Play Follow the Liter

Let's correlate a number to the addition of a single liter of air to the ocean. We realize that water will fall through bubbles whether the sea is calm or not. A liter of air could be seen as 1,000,000-cubic millimeter bubbles at the bottom of the sea. It would take .01 seconds for a single cubic millimeter of water to fall through this bubble. Since the diameter of a cubic millimeter sphere is about 1.25 millimeters, this small bubble would be displaced 800 times per meter of depth, or 8 seconds per meter. A larger cubic centimeter bubble would rise 1 meter in 2.55 seconds. Let's estimate that the average bubble rises 1 meter in 3.5 seconds. That ends up around 28.5 centimeters or 285 millimeters of bubble rise per second. Every bubble acts independently, but a little geometry shows us that each liter of air allows 285 liters of water to fall every second. These liters would otherwise be pushing forward in a tsunami. A tsunami wave takes 18 minutes to pass a point in the ocean. Consequently, 1-liter of air released just before the wave reaches a point, would end up mitigating the energy of 307,800 liters of water during its trip to the surface. But that's not all! A volume of gas in 200 meters of water (20 bar) grows to 20 times as large at the surface. The average volume of the rising bubble in this example is 3.6 times its initial volume.

The Multiple Is

I submit that a single liter of air, allowed to flow freely thru a tsunami wave, will mitigate 1,000,000 liters of lateral energy before that energy can push 1000 cubic meters of seawater up onto the shore. This math leads me to conclude that a precisely timed release of 1000 cubic meters of pressurized air, at a sufficient depth, ahead of an oncoming tsunami wave, would render the wave impotent.

The Sideways Proof

We've already seen, and it's common sense, that most of the water pressure existing in the heart of a tsunami wave is from the mass of the water. In other words, the water pressure at 200 meters, when there is no tsunami, would be 20 bar. The pressure at 200 meters of depth during a tsunami could be 20.05 bar. There isn't an additional half meter of water on the surface. There is a half meter of additional wave height caused by the bunching of ocean water. The leading edge of the wave meets water of normal pressure, and lifts that water's pressure by .05 bar. The wave keeps that pressure up for 18 minutes until it passes by, and the water then returns to normal pressure. If we're tracking the wave at 200 meters of depth, the leading edge of the wave is now 151 kilometers further along. During this 18 minutes, every liter, cubic meter or drop of water was being pushed from behind while pushing ahead.

A Newton's cradle demonstrates energy transfer. If we had a cradle with 9 balls, 8 of which weighed 50 grams and 1 weighed 40 grams, we'd notice that no matter where we place the lighter ball the pendulum motion would soon stop. It's fair to assume that only 80% of the energy can pass through that underweight ball. If we put air into the water ahead of a tsunami it would not lower the pressure of the water at depth, as the air would have the same pressure as its surroundings. It would instead reduce the mass or the "hardness" of the water and thus reduce the efficiency of the energy transfer. Think of baseball and aluminum bats versus wooden ones.

Now we'll do some arithmetic. We know that a wave exerting 20.05 bar of pressure at the 200-meter mark, and 30.05 bar at 300 meters will transfer its energy to the normal pressure water ahead of it, which will, in turn, send that energy forward. We also know that this energy transfer will occur over every plane of ocean between the initial disturbance and the shore. There will be no additional energy added to the wave on the way, and by the time it hits land, the sea near the quake will have settled down. We know that thousands of cubic kilometers of ocean are involved in transferring the wave energy, but we're only concerned about a net forward motion of 1 cubic kilometer that could end up on land.

If we put 1000 cubic meters of air in the water at some point, and manage to keep it underwater for the 18 minutes of the wave's passage, we can reduce the lateral flow to nearly nothing.

In this example, I'll use 100 kilometers of beachfront that we want to protect. The seafloor is 200 meters below and I'll use a 1 centimeter plane which the wave energy has to cross. This plane contains 200,000 cubic meters of water. Releasing 1000 cubic meters of air into this plane means it is now .5% air. Since the wave has not gotten to this point yet, the pressure of the water is the normal 1 bar per 10 meters. The air released also has this pressure at every depth. As the wave approaches, it easily passes through every 1 centimeter thick plane, and pressurizes the water by an additional .05 bar. At this bubble curtain the wave hits a snag. It cannot pressurize the 1 centimeter plane beyond our curtain until it pressurizes the air in our infused plane. None of the water will be pressurized until the air is. At 200 meters the air is at 20 bar of pressure. The wave will seek to increase the air and water pressure by .05 bar. The 1000 cubic meters of air we released in the water becomes 20,000 cubic meters near the surface. The average volume of air in the water would be 3600-cubic meters. The average pressure from 200 meters to the surface would be 3.6 bar. Before the 1 centimeter plane beyond our air infused section can have its pressure increased, the section we've just aerated must have its pressure raised. Before the average pressure can be increased to 3.65 bar, it must be increased to 3.61 bar.

Here's the math for figuring the amount of energy, also known as water pressure and volume, that would be required to raise the pressure of this 1 centimeter plane .01 bar. We're worried about 1 billion cubic meters being sent forward by the wave. During a tsunami wave, a 1 centimeter thick plane, 100 kilometers wide and 200 meters deep, would carry 208 cubic meters of excess forward energy. That figure comes from the observation that the wavelength is 48 kilometers. To raise the gas pressure from 3.6 to 3.61 bar you'd have to shrink the volume by 0.28%. That would be a 10-cubic meter reduction in the area occupied by the air, which would mean 10 more cubic meters of water would be in this space. This math would mean something if the 1000 cubic meters of compressed air were in a balloon tethered to the seafloor. In the real world, the air would be rising constantly despite any attempt to alter that course.

The 1000-cubic meters of air released at 200 meters of depth would have a pressure of 20 bar. There are three ways to raise the average pressure of this 1 centimeter plane by .01 bar. 1) Raise the pressure of the entire plane, air and water together. 2) Increase the water pressure enough to overwhelm the air. 3) Purge enough air to make it irrelevant in the average pressure of the plane.

If the oncoming wave is a dangerous one, that is to say one containing 1 billion-cubic meters of excess energy, each 1-centimeter plane would contain 208 cubic meters of net shoreward energy. Just 6 of these planes (or 6 centimeters of the wave) would be enough to fill the space occupied by the air, and then some. At this point, we are 6 centimeters into the wave and none of the leading edge has been able to get past this narrow plane. It has so far succeeded in occupying the space formerly occupied by the billions of bubbles that comprise the 1000 cubic meters. The air bubbles, which now occupy a bit more space and have a bit less pressure, are doing nothing to add to the overall pressure of this plane. The plane is maintaining its original average pressure of 3.6 bar, which is the same pressure as the plane ahead of it. The bubbles are nothing but an indicator of the pressure of the water. For them to exert an increasing pressure on the surrounding water, they would have to float downward!

Now, let's look at the situation 9 minutes, or halfway into the wave, to see how much progress is being made in increasing the pressure of this 1 centimeter plane. Since this is a large wave, half a billion cubic meters of excess lateral energy will have flowed into this plane in 9 minutes. The bubbles have risen to 100 meters of depth and now occupy 2000 cubic meters and have 10 bar of pressure. The 1000 cubic meters of air could have started out as 1000 meters, by 1000 meters, by 1 millimeter. That means that every millimeter of bubble rise equals 1000-cubic meters. These bubbles have taken a 100-meter trip from the seafloor to the halfway mark. They have created, and the wave has filled, 150,000,000-cubic meters of space with water. The extra 50,000,000 is from air expansion.

At first glance we would look at that and say it's still a powerful wave, an extra .035 bar of pressure being moved ahead. Let's look a little further. Due to the tsunami, the 200,000 cubic meters of water in the plane crashing into our treated plane "feels like" 200,208 cubic meters. Normally that extra energy would be passed along. However, since there are 1000-cubic meters of air in our bubble curtain, the next 1 centimeter plane in line would "feel like" it's being hit with 199,208 metric tons of weight! Notice how I use mass and weight and volume and energy interchangeably! The lighter column could not pass its energy efficiently to its heavier neighbor. That would be tantamount to expecting a rubber hammer to do the same work as a steel one.

The obvious question here is: "Would this analysis be the same for a different size plane?" My answer is that wave energy is not passed on one centimeter at a time. Rather, it's more of a molecule to molecule energy transfer. Any size plane would represent the concept, but the smallest plane imaginable would be the closest to the actual mechanics of the idea. Since we're talking about kinetic energy being absorbed instead of diverted, the closer we can get to a several-molecule-wide plane, the better.

Believe Your Eyes

Anyone who has ever seen an ocean wave wash up on a beach has seen the effect of air on the wave. The last moments of a wave's lifespan are the moments when it contains a tremendous amount of air. Typically, as a wave approaches shallow water the top curls over its base and falls into the rest of itself. This action causes splashing and generates bubbles which are included in the weakening wave. If the theory that air bubbles can mitigate wave energy is correct, we would expect to see the very thing we do see when a wave hits the beach.

My understanding is that America was blessed with the natural coast protection of "the Oceans, white with foam". At least that's how Irving Berlin put it.

Figure 7—A Wave Dies Out Near the Beach

My Theory—The Top Passes the Bottom

Remember the formula for wave velocity from chapter 2? V = the square root of D / 9.81? In shallow water a small difference in depth would lead to a significant difference in velocity. Consider a 1 meter tall wave in 3 meters of water. The math shows us that this wave is traveling at just over 33 meters a minute. A 3 and ½ meter tall wave would travel at nearly 36 meters per minute. A 4-meter-tall wave travels at over 38 meters per minute. This means that a 4-meter-tall wave would pass its 3-meter-tall base by over 1 meter every 12 seconds.

From the beach, we don't see this happen, because it doesn't. What we see is the 4-meter wave top fall into the trailing base once there's no support for its height. The splash pumps air into the wave and it quickly disintegrates.

I believe releasing air into a wave from below would have the same effect as splashing air into it from above. I believe both forms of air infusion would cause the wave to disintegrate.

CHAPTER FIVE

Am I Serious?

It seems irrational to believe that tsunami mitigation can be so simple and therefore inexpensive. How can something as simple as air have such a profound effect on something as powerful as a tsunami? Air is already used as insulation, to keep people from crashing through the windshield in auto wrecks, and to keep jetliners aloft. Involving air in a moving tsunami wave has to disrupt its nearly perfect efficiency. I can accept the ratio presented earlier.

The current response to tsunamis is to save people with evacuations and property with seawalls. Granted, if the seawalls work, people would also be saved. Unfortunately, there's no guarantee the seawalls will hold. In the case of a 10-meter wave, an 8-meter seawall is not 80% effective, it's closer to 0%. Also in the case of a 10-meter-high wave, preparing for it with a 15-meter-high seawall is not 25% more effective than a 12-meter-high wall. Evacuations are called for so often but needed so seldom that there's a strong skepticism that such action is necessary. Sadly, there have been incidents where people have heard the warnings, gone to the seaside for a better look, and been killed by the wave. Having said that, it's still a wonderful thing that tsunami forecasting has come so far in the last half century. Without those improvements, no new approach would be feasible.

A solution involving mitigating the wave while it's still at sea is superior to the current procedures in several obvious ways. First, it's somewhat portable. After setting up the basic infrastructure we need only activate it when and where it's needed. Second, it can be partially successful. Unlike seawalls, which are hit-or-miss structures, the "air" approach can do some good even missing the mark. If your goal is to reduce a wave by 75% and you end up reducing it by just 15% this would be considered a qualified success! Third, there's no problem with overkill. Let's say we're prepared for an event like the meteor strike in the movie "Deep Impact" but all we get is a Superstorm Sandy. Most folks wouldn't consider it to be a misfortune to be unable to use an insurance policy. Finally, the cost has to be much less. I'm certain we could pump a lot of air into the ocean for the $27 million Japan spends on 1 mile of seawall. Even unnecessary evacuations are costly in lost productivity, transportation expenses, and the increased likelihood of looting. Necessary evacuations are not always believed to be so.

I once believed that if I came up with a scheme to reduce tsunami destruction by one half of 1%, no one would be impressed. I realize now that I was wrong. There is now a ratio of air volume placed in the ocean versus water ending up on the land (52,000 to 1). Although the real-world number may be completely different than the arithmetically derived number, the process is still revolutionary. To put it another way, it's easier and cheaper to put a cubic kilometer of air in the ocean ahead of and during a tsunami than it is to clean up a cubic kilometer of sea water from the land. This would be the amount of air necessary in a 1 to 1 ratio of air to water inundation.

Climate Science

Allow me to digress here for a bit. One of the most important branches of science these days is "Climate Science." Many of the world's most prominent scientists have taken a look at what modern life has done to the Earth's environment and have expressed concern. A widely-accepted theory is that if mankind doesn't reduce the amount of carbon that is being released into the atmosphere, there is a probability that temperatures will climb faster than they otherwise would. This, in turn, will bring about more unusual weather events and speed the melting of much of the world's ice, including the Greenland Ice Sheet. If the Greenland Ice Sheet melted or became floating sea ice, it would cause worldwide sea level rise of at least six meters. This could happen in the next 200 years or sooner. My theory is better than this theory in some significant ways, although they both refer to sea level rise.

Let's presume that both of our plans are adopted. They hope for results in 100 plus years, my plan could yield results in 100 minutes. They have no definitive results predicted, my plan would eliminate destructive tsunamis. Their plan has some prominent detractors, known as skeptics, critics and even "deniers", while no one has yet said my plan won't work. I'm still looking for my first critic or supporter. Finally, their plan requires people to stop doing something they're already doing, namely stop using so much fossil fuel. My plan requires people do something they're not now doing, namely put air ahead of a tsunami. A quick fix of an action seems so much easier than a long program of denial.

Even though it's very difficult to get the public to alter its behavior, especially when there is no instant gratification, science keeps up the effort. I understand how difficult it is for scientists to educate millions of laypeople on complicated concepts. My challenge is for a layman (me) to encourage scientist to consider a simple concept!

Climate Science has helped us learn about a way for society to ameliorate future problems by taking small steps today. They have persuaded policy makers that if most folks would reduce their carbon footprint, future problems could be less significant. I contend that if thousands of boat owners, beachfront homeowners and communities would each contribute a bit of mitigation, the results would be significant. Adding a small amount of air a few meters down into the wave couldn't do any harm. With enough contributors the goal of stopping tsunamis would be met!

Kitchen Sink Science

Here are some of the experiments I've performed to establish the efficacy of my approach. I've pumped flat water versus soda water into a container. The soda water takes significantly longer to accumulate. I've run water through multiple garden hoses, allowing one of the hoses to be empty of water. The longest time between the water flow being started, and the flow being at full force, comes when the empty hose is closest to the tap. I've pumped water into a closed flask of soda water, versus flat water, where the pressure in the flask forced the water out. Again, the flat water transferred the pumped water much more efficiently. There was even one ill-fated attempt involving a scuba tank, a camera on a boogie board, and my wife jumping into a pool to create a wave. Someone called security! All of these experiments worked out as expected.

The simplest experiment on this concept is one most of us did as children. Take a spray bottle or a squirt gun and see how long it takes to pump an ounce of water into a cup. Next, try again with soda water. This is one of those rare scientific experiments with no problem of replication!

Frankly, I believe seawalls and evacuations will soon be obsolete in responding to tsunamis. I believe this simple idea, or some version of this simple idea, can prevent tsunami destruction.

The fact that the energy from the tsunami wave must cross every plane of ocean between the disturbance and the shore, means that there are infinite places to interrupt the lateral flow. You could stop it in the bay or in the deep ocean. You could pump air into the water in multiple locations, and the effect would be cumulative.

CHAPTER SIX

"Braking" Waves

Here are some of the easier ways to introduce air or other gases into the water ahead of a wave:

Boats With Air Compressors

1) This device would consist of a hose dropped to a significant depth attached to an air compressor on a boat. My original idea was to hang an air hose over the side of a boat. A weighted hose with a high-pressure compressor would work quite well. The idea now is to equip any boat; coast guard, commercial or recreational, with a simple apparatus to help mitigate tsunamis when the need arises. The apparatus would consist of a tank, with a p trap drain, connected to a large length of weighted hose. Water would be pumped into the tank, while air would be pumped into the outflow hose beyond the p trap. The water would be pumped into a pool or tank at the top of the vessel. That water would be drained into the ocean to a depth of 300 meters (give or take). Just above the point where the drain hose hits the ocean surface, there would be a p trap to keep air from floating up the hose back to the pool. Downstream of the p trap would be a pump which would insert compressed air into the draining water flow. The quantity of air that could

be released into the ocean with this method is limited only by the pump and hose size.

The concept here would involve a network of willing boat owners whose ships could be located via GPS in an emergency. At that point, a message would be sent along the lines of "two large tsunami waves will be traveling through your point in the ocean beginning in 11 minutes. Please initiate mitigation procedures." Participants could be given a break on their insurance or a tax credit for providing this alternative to seawalls. There would be no practical limit to the amount of air that could be pumped into the ocean at depth, but even a single participating vessel pumping 20 liters of air (after being compressed to 10 bar) per minute to a depth of 100 meters would mitigate the lateral flow of a huge tsunami. Each 20 liters of air released at depth would expand on the way up, providing an average of 58.6 liters of mitigating air every second of its 319 second journey to the surface. This totals nearly 580,000 liters of water, in the heart of the wave, falling instead of pushing forward, using our previously established 31 to 1 ratio. If the pump continues to operate for the entire 18 minutes of the passing tsunami, we can expect a total of over 10,000 cubic meters of water which will not be pushed forward by the wave. This means that 5 meters of beachfront would see a reduction of 20% of the size of the wave. This may not seem significant when we're talking about hundreds of kilometers of shoreline which need to be protected. Also, I realize that you can't specifically protect a mere 5 meters of shoreline. However, this process would not involve just one pump. If one pump has a tiny impact on the tsunami wave it still has an impact! Thousands of these pumps would be sufficient to mitigate any tsunami!

Tanks of Air Dropped From Boats

2) Another mitigating protocol would be tanks of compressed air dropped overboard, with a pressure sensitive valve. This idea is for people who would like to participate in tsunami mitigation programs, but don't want hoses or pumps or large tanks on their vessel. The optimal situation for a single standard scuba tank would be for it to be dropped into deep water ten minutes before the leading edge of the tsunami reaches that point. The tank could be tethered to a long cord, or the participants could just take one for the team. The tank would have a valve as simple as a bicycle inner tube valve which would allow the tank to fill with water and expel the air once the water pressure had gotten to a certain point, perhaps 100 bar. Ideally, the first few seconds of wave flow would encounter 23 liters of rising air bubbles at 1000 meters. Thirty-two seconds later, these air bubbles would measure around 23 1/4 liters and exist in 990 meters of depth. The average size of this mass of rising bubbles for any given instance of its rise to the surface is 119 liters. This means that this one tank would provide the opportunity for nearly 4,000 cubic meters of water to fall instead of flow forward in a tsunami. Consequently, 250 of these tanks could reduce a wave by 1 meter over a hundred-kilometer shoreline.

Dedicated Air Pipeline

3) The first land-based idea is a dedicated air pipeline controlled from shore. This apparatus involves nothing but a long pipe, with a release valve at the end and an air pump at the beginning. This pipe could run alongside existing pipes or cables or sit on the ocean floor by itself. I envision this pipe being placed at the outer edge of a susceptible bay, and to

be used whenever the potential for a destructive wave arises. The volume of air which could be accommodated by such a system is infinite. The Langeled natural gas pipeline in the North Sea transports 25.5 billion cubic meters of natural gas every year over its length. That translates to 808 cubic meters a second. A pipe releasing that much air (or natural gas for that matter) would put over 872,000 cubic liters of air in the water, mitigating 27 million cubic meters of tsunami flow per second. This would protect 3000 kilometers of coastline from any tsunami generated from a point beyond this apparatus. A more likely scenario would be to place pipes with one tenth the capacity every 300 kilometers or so. The great advantage of this method it that it could be employed during tsunamis, storm surges, hurricanes or just to mitigate shore erosion.

Tanks Stored on the Ocean Floor

4) A variation of the previous idea is large tanks of compressed air stationed under water. I liked this method so much, I applied for a "patent pending." It would protect a bay or a riverbed from tsunamis. There might be some difficulty keeping it operational, as it would be submerged in deep water all of the time. These tanks would have to have some sort of remote control valve and regular maintenance to insure they would be ready in an emergency.

Depth Charges

5) The quickest way to release gas into the ocean would be depth charges. They would instantly turn solid explosives to gas. This would be a quick fix for a tsunami occurring before

any of the other methods are put in place. The amount of gas created by a conventional explosion is a known value. Care would have to be used to prevent damage to marine life or submarines. Bombing an area ahead of a wave would have the advantages of all of the other methods of putting gas in the ocean. Plus it would have the additional benefit of creating some tsunami mitigation, created by the counter energy of the explosion.

Retrofit Current Infrastructure

6) Retrofit Current Infrastructure.

The legend of King Canute is well known to those interested in sea related folklore. The story goes like this. In the early 11th century there lived a monarch known as King Canute. He was a wise king who was perturbed by his sycophantic court flattering him beyond all reason. One day, after hearing how powerful he was, he asked his court if they believed he was powerful enough to stop the waves. Not wishing to doubt their king's power his court quickly agreed that if he wanted to, he could stop the waves. King Canute decided to perform an experiment on his powerfulness. He went to the shore with his court and commanded the waves to stop! When the waves failed to heed his orders, as he knew they would, he had demonstrated that while his power was great, it was not as great as God's.

Since those days, many events formerly thought to be exclusively in God's hands have been tamed a bit by science. I believe that tsunami waves are next in line for some human tinkering.

Since most coastal municipalities have pipelines pumping large amounts of treated waste water deep into the sea, it would be a simple process to pump carbon dioxide, oxygen, nitrogen or simply air into this flowing stream. These outflow pipes are controlled by the public and could easily be retrofitted with pumps to infuse the wastewater with compressed air. The wastewater pipe for Los Angeles ends 7 miles out to sea, and pumps millions of gallons of water an hour into the ocean. A liter of water can hold several liters of surface pressure air or other gas, as is the case with carbonated beverages. The amount of air that could be pumped to the ocean floor using this method would be virtually without limit. Once a threatening earthquake occurred, the local authorities could flip a switch. Thousands of cubic meters of air would be quickly released at the ocean floor and a disaster would be averted. Like King Canute, the local Mayor would demand that the waves stop. But unlike the situation with the ancient King, the waves will obey!

Figure 8—Mayor Canute Re-enacts His Heroic Act—Saving the Town of Port Dockport Beach

CHAPTER SEVEN

We Look at Tsunamis Differently

When I used to look at mazes as a kid, I found it was always quite simple to look at the goal and work backwards. That's the way I look at tsunamis. Instead of thinking about the size of seawall needed to stop a 10-meter wave, I think of how much water is required to create one. I don't theorize about how large an earthquake need be to create a tsunami. (The scientists who figured this out are brilliant. I'm awed by them!) I look, rather, at the amount of lateral energy traveling across the ocean and up onto the shore. The whole idea of lateral energy doesn't appear in the literature, but it's a logical concept that differentiates tsunamis from tides and every day waves. There has to be an unusual amount of lateral energy in a tsunami or the wave would do nothing but bob up and down across the ocean. It's like the middle ball of a Newton's Cradle, it doesn't move much but the energy is passing through. There was a western movie hero in the 1940s and 50s who went by the name "Lash LaRue." His unique attribute was that he was proficient with a bullwhip, so much so that he gave Harrison Ford lessons in its use for the Indiana Jones movies. (There have been attempts during my lifetime by acquaintances to attach that sobriquet to me, attempts which I successfully resisted!) A bullwhip acts something like a wave, the energy is initiated at one end and travels in a wave motion. The thing about a 20-foot-long bullwhip is that no matter how fearsome the cracking of the whip appears, if you're 25 feet away you have nothing to worry about. If, however, old "Lash" moved about 6 feet closer, you could be in trouble. The same is true of a tsunami wave. All the motion of millions of cubic kilometers of water will only be a problem if part of that water gets up on land. Obviously, all the water is not just moving up and down, some of it must be moving toward the shore.

Finally, I like to slice and dice the tsunami wave to make it easier to contemplate. I find it comfortable thinking of liters versus cubic meters rather than a few cubic kilometers versus thousands. Here, I make the defensible assumption that the energy traveling through the wave is homogeneous. It's logical to believe that if one cube of water in the wave is carrying 16 grams of flowing energy, its neighbor cube will be doing likewise. I can think of nothing that would make one section of wave noticeably different than another.

Earlier, I talked about 3-cubic kilometers of lateral energy and promoted a goal of reducing that by 1-cubic kilometer. It's quite possible that this base of 2-cubic kilometers is way off, but that really doesn't matter. We're solely interested in keeping the cubic kilometer that causes damage from being pushed onto land in the first place. It's obvious that a 20% reduction in a 10-meter wave would lead to an 8-meter wave. An 8-meter wave would be destructive, but it would reveal some progress in mitigation. Knowing that we have the ability to reduce a wave means that we have the ability to stop a wave. That which was deemed "impossible" is not only possible, but simple!

Among the many things about tsunami waves that I don't fully understand is the concept of gravity waves. I've read that a gravity wave (such as a tsunami) is the process of regaining equilibrium between the atmosphere and the sea, or a dense fluid and a less dense one. To get a better handle on this concept I thought I'd look at the speed of a falling object, to see gravity's affect.

My Theory—Wave Speed Vs. a Falling Object

If you dropped a bowling ball (or a water bottle or a feather for that matter) in a vacuum from a height of 7000 meters, you'd see it constantly accelerate at the rate of 9.81 meters per second squared, until it hit the ground. Since 7000 divided by 9.81 is 713.5, we know that 713.5 is the square of the number of seconds this item would take to fall to the ground. The square root of 713.5 is 26.7. That means the object will hit the ground in 26.7 seconds. The average speed of this fall would be just over 262 meters per second (7000 divided by 26.7). Another way to look at 262 meters per second is 943 kilometers per hour. If this number seems familiar you, read the chart on tsunami velocity carefully. The same calculations work for all depths. What this tells us is that a cubic meter of water at the top of the wave (or a cubic kilometer, or the whole wave) falls forward at the same average speed as it would fall down if it could. Of course, it can't fall down. There's water there. And it really can't fall forward either. There's water there too. What it can do is pass its energy into the water ahead of it. The water ahead of it won't move either, but it will pass its energy along at the rate of 943 kilometers per hour. Remember this is at 7000 meters of ocean depth. As the wave moves to shallower water the velocity and wavelength size lessen. The time it takes the wave to pass a point in the water remains at 18 minutes. The spheres referenced earlier keep spinning, sending some energy away from the earthquake and some energy back toward it. The net energy, which can also be measured in liters or cubic meters, will be away from the quake. The total energy being transferred by the tsunami wave will be less than the amount of water displaced by the disturbance, and more than the amount of water brought up on shore. A single point disturbance, such as a meteor, would generate energy in a circle. A nearby shore lying in, say, an 18-degree arc from the meteor strike could be hit by no more than 5% of the total water displaced. This is because 18^0 is 5% of 360^0. An earthquake that travels along a line (like the Indian Ocean earthquake) can carry nearly half its energy to a shore on a parallel line to the quake.

In the case of the Indian Ocean Tsunami, there weren't many barriers absorbing the energy of the wave. Madagascar protected some of the African Coast, but mostly the wave was weakened by distance. I've read that the wave could still be detected after an entire trip around the world! Also, I've seen one estimate that 30-cubic kilometers of water was displaced by the quake. Since water is essentially incompressible, that 30-cubic kilometers had to displace another 30-cubic kilometers and so on until some of the water was displaced onto a shore. Since air *is* compressible, I conclude that some of the tsunami wave energy would be spent compressing it. The wave could not compress air and push its energy forward at the same time.

It also seems logical to conclude that one large bubble of air will absorb the same energy as many small bubbles, provided the total mass is the same.

Next, I'd like to compare two waves of equal size and depth. The difference would be, one would be a regular tsunami wave, and the other an air-treated wave.

An Untouched Wave

Let's look first at a wave heading toward a beach unimpeded. Suppose this wave contains 2-cubic kilometers of excess energy and is heading toward 200 kilometers of beach. At 50 meters of depth the wavelength is 23 kilometers. A 200-kilometer-wide section of this wave would comprise 2300 cubic kilometers of water. The 2-cubic kilometers of excess energy flowing toward the beach would be less than 0.1% of the wave. Once it gets to 10 meters of depth, the wavelength would have shrunk to 10.6 kilometers. The lateral flow would be close to 10% of the wave by then. Now, with almost 10% of the water near the shore being displaced by the lateral flow of the tsunami, it has nowhere to go but up on the land. A single wave will push enough water up on land to inundate 1000 square kilometers of land in 18 minutes.

Tiny Bubbles

Now for the second wave, let's try something different. Suppose there's a pipe that can pump 100-cubic meters of compressed air into the bottom of this section of ocean as quickly as is necessary. Suppose it starts pumping before the wave gets to this point, and continues to pump for the duration of the wave. Let's say it takes each 10-cubic meter bubble 4 minutes to rise to the surface. By the time it gets to the surface it's a 50-cubic meter bubble. This means there will be four large bubbles at various depths during every second of the wave passing this point, previously shown to be 18 minutes in total. To make the math simple, let's say we'll look at 100-cubic meters of air at a time. This would more likely exist as 100 million-cubic centimeters. This air would stay in the water for the duration of the wave. A 100-cubic meter theoretical void would be filled with 100-cubic meters of water. That would absorb 100-cubic meters of the oncoming lateral energy. A void would absorb this energy one time. Bubbles of the same total size would absorb the same energy on the bottom 1-centimeter of wave, and then do the same to the next centimeter. Over 200 meters it would repeat this process 20,000 times. The arithmetic reveals that if you could release 100 cubic meters of air 50 times into a wave, all of the energy of that wave would be mitigated.

This entire process is more impressive if you estimate that the bubbles are going to be 1-cubic millimeter in volume. Plus, you can take into account that the volume of the gas will expand as it rises to the surface. Once we establish a number, we can adjust the volume of air necessary to attain the desired results. If we over-estimate the amount of air necessary, no harm will be done. Imagine a situation where there wasn't going to be a tsunami in any case. With an over-abundance of caution, we release 1-cubic-kilometer of air into the deep sea. Half an hour later, everything would be back to normal, none the worse for wear.

CHAPTER EIGHT

The Aleutian Earthquake of 1946

On April 1, 1946, a large earthquake occurred 150 kilometers off the coast of Unimak Island, the largest island in the Aleutian chain. A short time after the earthquake, a 45-meter-tall tsunami wave hit the island and destroyed a lighthouse, the base of which sat at 30 meters above sea level. All five lighthouse workers died. Four hours later, the tsunami wave hit Hilo on the Island of Hawaii and claimed another 160 lives. I contend that today's technology would not only be able to save Hilo from the death and destruction that occurred that day, but it would also be able to save those closer to the earthquake, such as the men on Unimak Island.

Scientists have wondered how this strong, but not extremely strong earthquake could have caused so much damage. In 2004 scientists conducted sea floor mapping to see if they could find evidence of a large underwater landslide which coincided with the earthquake, that would help explain the outsized tsunami that followed. They found none. Other scientists have hypothesized that the original measurements were incorrect, or that the wave rumbled in a certain way to mask its true size. I have my own way of looking at it. The mystery *could* be explained as follows:

My Theory: The 1946 Tsunami.

Unimak Island was so close to the epicenter of the quake that the wave had not formed completely, it was just water sloshing around a disturbance. If the depth of the ocean here was 4000 meters, the first wavelength is 213 kilometers. If the wave on the Unimak side of the quake was 35 meters tall (it is said), and 15 kilometers from side to side, and perhaps involving the front 10 kilometers of the wave, then over 5-cubic kilometers of water must have risen out of the ocean and inundated a coast of the island. A lighthouse sitting on a 30-meter-tall hill implies the topography was quite steep. This means the water would have fallen back down very quickly, catching up to the southbound wave and causing more problems for Hawaii. Additionally, isn't it possible that the rotation of the Earth and centrifugal force encourage the southbound water to move toward the equator?

We Could Have Done Better

Even though the 1946 disaster was the deadliest tsunami in Hawaii's history, the damage could have been prevented with the release of a few thousand cubic meters of air into the waters of Hilo Bay. Saving the lighthouse on Unimak Island would have been more difficult. However, it still would have been feasible! Accepting for a moment the idea that 5-cubic kilometers of water washed up on the shores of the island, we must merely think of a way to divert that much water. At 713 kilometers-per-hour, the leading edge of the tsunami would cover 150 kilometers in 12 and 1/2 minutes. The back end would arrive 18 minutes later. Let's say we prepared for this possibility by placing two pipes, each capable of releasing 2-cubic meters of air a second into the water at 300 meters of depth. It would take around 15 minutes for this air to rise to the surface. Let's also stipulate that we could get the pumps working within 10 minutes of an earthquake. The 2-cubic meters would turn into 60-cubic meters at the surface, due to lower water pressure. A continuous flow would mean each pipe would be providing 7200 cubic meters of air bubbles that would run interference into the tsunami as the wave approached the bubble curtain. Since there would be two pipes, that system would be providing 14.4 billion cubic centimeters of air bubbles, all providing an opportunity for the lateral 5-cubic kilometers of wave energy to fall down, instead of pushing forward. Each centimeter of the onrushing wave would carry nearly 847 cubic meters of energy, pushing the water ahead of it forward. When that onrushing lateral energy meets the 14,400 cubic meters of endless air bubbles, the danger to the lighthouse would end. Since the water wouldn't be climbing the shores of Unimak Island, it would not add to the southbound wave.

CHAPTER NINE

Seawalls are Sometimes
Worse Than Nothing

Those of us who have seen videos of the horrific Japan Tsunami of 2011 couldn't help but think they should build more seawalls. The water kept rising in the harbor, eventually topping the tide gate, and continued to rise and spread up the roads then through buildings, tossing vehicles and debris around like leaves. I estimated the flow inland to be around 10 kilometers an hour, too fast for most to outrun, especially because the straight path away from the sea was usually unavailable. Aside from the fact that over 90% of Japan's seawalls failed during this tsunami, representing billions of dollars of wasted infrastructure spending, let's consider whether a failed seawall was better or worse than nothing at all.

Suppose you could see the future and knew that a 10-meter tsunami was going to strike a 10-kilometer shoreline in 6 months. Being responsible, and a bit overly enthusiastic, you get your town to build a 12-meter seawall 10 kilometers wide, 250 meters from the high tide line. Six months later the 10-meter wave hits, the seawall stands firm, and everyone cheers, because a wave that was going to travel 2 kilometers inland and inundate everything in its path was stopped near the beach!! Folks see the beginning of the wave stop at the wall. The cheering continues as the wave continues to pump ocean water onto the beach between the shore and the seawall. Unfortunately, after the cheering stops the wave doesn't recede. In fact, the water continues to rise. After 6 minutes the rising water reaches the top of our new seawall and starts flowing over. After 10 minutes the entire wall fails and the one third of the wave that was being stacked up on the beach falls ahead, not at a runner's speed, but at the speed of a dam bursting. At this point all of the water that was going to move ahead has some catching up to do.

The other thing about seawalls is they have to end somewhere. Suppose you built a 500-kilometer wall that covered 90% of your shoreline. If a tsunami did occur, the wall would divert much of the wave energy and flooding to the uncovered 10%. There are also riverbeds, dock access roads and beachfront houses which make a long seawall partially unfeasible.

Had we instead attempted a deep-water method of tsunami mitigation it may not have worked. But it almost goes without saying that an ocean-based mitigation effort cannot do more harm than good.

CHAPTER TEN

Storm Surges

Wave Trains

Some of the worst natural disasters in the history of the world have been caused by storm surges. Hundreds of thousands of people have perished in recorded history due to these waves brought ashore by high winds. In 1900, a hurricane hit Galveston, Texas and killed over 6,000 people. The storm surge did most of the damage.

A storm surge is similar to a tsunami in effect, but not in its cause. In a storm surge, a large low pressure system actually lifts a section of ocean in a bulge, allowing the high winds to grab the water and create a wave train. As the wind blows, the waves get higher, which allows more surface area to get caught in the wind, and leads to larger waves. Just like a tsunami, a storm surge is mostly water moving up and down in a wave-like motion. If there is no shoreline close by, as is usually the case, the waves calm down when the winds die down. When there is land nearby, especially during a high tide, the results can be devastating.

Storm surge waves are never just a single wave, like a tsunami, rather they must occur in groups. Sets of waves hitting the beach are the norm, and storm surges differ from normal wave sets by magnitude and timing.

When we see a set of, say, 7 waves coming toward the shore, they may look like 7 different events, but they are the product of a single event. The waves move with one another. If you could stop the lead wave, you'd stop the rest of them. More to the point, if you could decrease each wave's magnitude by 14% you'd weaken the entire set by enough to turn it into a common event, as opposed to a flood.

How do I get this number? It's mostly an educated guess based on Typhoon Haiyan which devastated the Philippines in November of 2013. This typhoon created a storm surge which sent waves up to nearly 6 meters in height up to 1 kilometer inland. The death toll in the Philippines from the typhoon and storm surge was over 6,000. Assume the average wave height was 5 meters. Let's use some geometry to figure the total inundation over 100 kilometers of shoreline. Inundating land 1 kilometer inward to an elevation of 5 meters would take 250 million cubic meters. Unlike a tsunami, wind driven waves don't affect the ocean from floor to surface. Let's say these waves' energy is mostly confined to the top 10 meters of ocean water. Also, the heart of the storm reaches out 3 kilometers to sea. That means 3 billion cubic meters of ocean water are involved in this storm surge. A 14% reduction in wave energy would translate to 420 million cubic meters less water that could be churned up toward the land.

Saving Lives

The methods discussed earlier in this book to mitigate tsunamis can easily be used to mitigate storm surges. Air, released on the ocean floor, will become large bubbles near the surface, and will tend to weaken the waves that could turn into a storm surge. Even if the bulk of the wave's energy is carried in the top 3 meters of the ocean, every bubble released from the seafloor would still affect the wave for 10 seconds or so.

There are two ways an air release could mitigate a forming storm surge. First, air could cause the waves to break prematurely, folding even more air under the leading edge of each wave, and leading to a weaker wave. Second, aerating the water will provide less of an opportunity for the low-pressure system to lift up the sea surface. This will lead to a weaker wave in the first place. For a home experiment of how this works try this: Get a large drinking straw and drink some water out of a glass. Next, try the same thing with a carbonated drink! You'll find that the low-pressure system you create with your drinking straw is more efficient picking up flat water than the same system is in lifting your carbonated beverage!

CHAPTER ELEVEN

Hurricanes

It occurred to me that a better way to stop storm surges than pumping air into the forming waves is to weaken the wind that causes them in the first place. This would have the added benefit of diminishing all of the damage which a hurricane can cause. At the risk of being accused of having an answer for everything, and it's always the same answer, consider this:

Hurricanes form as tropical storms and then either grow or die. The things that will cause a hurricane to grow are, among others, distance from the equator, an ocean underneath and temperatures of the surface water of 80° or more. Things that will cause the hurricane to weaken are land, cold water or wind shear. A hurricane can gain significant strength by traveling over a warm ocean on a hot day and collecting millions of tons of energizing water vapor.

Water vapor is lighter than air. When the surface temperature of the ocean is over 80° Fahrenheit the conditions exist to feed a hurricane. The warm water must exist below the surface to a depth of 50 meters. Air being pumped deep into the ocean typically encounters temperatures under 35° Fahrenheit. Air pumped to 300 meters would quickly transfer its heat to the cold water. When these bubbles reached the 50-meter mark they would absorb heat from the warm water. If you've ever taken a bath in a jetted tub you've seen how room temperature air bubbles can lower the temperature of a large amount of water quite quickly. The bubbles released at the ocean floor spend over 90% of their trip to the surface in temperatures below 35° Fahrenheit. As is true for this whole book, a small amount of air released may not do much good, but we can always increase the volume!

The math here seems fairly straightforward, but I don't think I need to get into a long analysis of cooling a portion of the ocean in a book about tsunami mitigation. I'll just say that an average hurricane has a diameter of perhaps 300 miles. If you wanted to cool some of the water under a portion of the storm, you could dispatch ships to pump air beneath the ocean in the southern part of the wave. A few hundred meters down, the air would be released in 35° water. If that air rises to encounter an 81° water temperature near the surface it will warm considerably. The heat in those bubbles will have come from the water. It is clear that enough air cooling of the water will weaken the potential hurricane.

There is also a potential for scientists to figure out a way to use a small area of cooler ocean water to steer a developing storm. I know this could be risky, as no one would want to make a situation worse by steering a storm to land. However, the potential benefit is worth a look.

There could be a simple explanation why none of this would do any good. Perhaps I'll hear about it.

CHAPTER TWELVE

Rogue Waves

Another potential application of a ship-based air pump would be to help stabilize the vessel in stormy seas. Upon detecting an approaching rogue wave, the system could quickly release an "air curtain" of bubbles around the ship. This would weaken the wave through the area occupied by the ship and lessen the effect of the wave's impact. I believe this system could be deployed during the duration of a storm. This would make the already low risk of sailing through stormy seas even less so.

A simple experiment to prove the effectiveness of such a system can be done with a long garden hose. Open a faucet connected to a garden hose filled with water and measure the time before water is flowing out the other end at full pressure. Next, allow a foot of air to get into the hose near the tap and repeat the experiment. Full pressure flow will not be achieved until the air is purged!

CHAPTER THIRTEEN

Summary and More Analogies

This book began with the premise that if you put air in front of a tsunami it would weaken the wave. That's a simple concept that takes a few seconds to explain. The rest of this book was conceptualizing the forces at play. I'll summarize them now.

A tsunami begins as a sudden and large displacement of water. That displacement forms a wave which transfers energy, unabated, through the medium, which is usually an ocean. After the wave is formed, there will be no more energy added to it as it travels across the sea. The wave continues long after the original disturbance has calmed down. No water is added to or subtracted from the ocean during the wave's journey. It doesn't take much energy to make a wave. It takes much more to move water. (To prove this, fill a bowl with water and drop it a half inch to see a wave. Now try emptying that bowl using the same force.) Most of the energy in the wave merely moves it up and down. There is some lateral energy which will flood a coastal area if not abated.

Putting air in front of the wave at any point weakens the lateral energy. It gives that energy a path of less resistance compared to pushing ahead. The energy will either push down instead of ahead by dropping through bubbles, or be expended "trying" to compress air in its path. Either way, the forward energy of the wave will be diminished.

We know intuitively that pouring a large amount of water into the ocean over a reasonably short period of time will not cause a wave. The Amazon river sends 209,000 cubic meters per second into the Atlantic Ocean with no dangerous wave resulting. My belief is that the tumult of the flowing water allows the ocean to accommodate the inflow without a problem. An addition of air underwater is like adding tumult without adding water. The bubbles slowly move water a bit in every direction and the energy coming from behind is equally dispersed. The bubles go straight up and the energy goes where it can.

A downhill runaway truck ramp provides a good analogy to my way of thinking. Occasionally, brakes fail on large trucks. If the truck is traveling downhill this will often result in a fatal crash. Highway engineers have put some runaway truck ramps off the road for these events. On a downhill slope, these ramps consist of a stretch of road surface of sand and gravel. At the end of the stretch are barrels filled with water and sand. The sand on the road is supposed to slow the truck, and the barrels at the end are supposed to stop it. This works sometimes. My idea is similar. You mitigate some of the energy of a tsunami before it crashes into a final wall!

I owe a debt to the folks involved in climate science. They advocate that millions of ordinary people can do things a bit differently and improve our environment. This bottom up approach works with tsunami mitigation. If 10,000 boat owners or beachfront property owners could act quickly after an earthquake, their environment would be impacted less.

Now I'll go back to talking about scale one last time:

If you had to deal with a runaway freight train that was neither gaining nor losing momentum you could stop it with a ball of string. You'd merely have to place a length of string around two trees and over the track and wait for the train to run into it. It would take some of the momentum out of the rolling train to break the string, so you'd have to do it quite a few times. With a large enough ball of string, you could get it done.

CHAPTER FOURTEEN

An Apology and a Thank-You

I came up with this idea a few years ago but didn't write about it. Instead, I shared it with friends and family until they got tired of hearing about it. If the idea has merit, I apologize for not presenting it earlier. If it has none, I apologize for presenting it at all!

I'd like to thank Balboa Press for publishing this book and YOU for reading it. I have confidence that this idea has merit and believe that a new industry will grow up around it. It will be quite a relief in the near future when we can just tell a Tsunami WAVE "GOODBYE!"

www.ingramcontent.com/pod-product-compliance
Lightning Source LLC
Chambersburg PA
CBHW050430290526
45786CB00003B/1473